EMMANUEL JOSEPH

The Quiet Hustle, Achieving More by Slowing Down and Connecting Deeply

Copyright © 2025 by Emmanuel Joseph

All rights reserved. No part of this publication may be reproduced, stored or transmitted in any form or by any means, electronic, mechanical, photocopying, recording, scanning, or otherwise without written permission from the publisher. It is illegal to copy this book, post it to a website, or distribute it by any other means without permission.

First edition

This book was professionally typeset on Reedsy. Find out more at reedsy.com

Contents

1	Chapter 1: The Noise of Modern Life	1
2	Chapter 2: Embracing Stillness	3
3	Chapter 3: The Power of Deep Work	4
4	Chapter 4: Cultivating Presence	6
5	Chapter 5: The Art of Single-Tasking	7
6	Chapter 6: Building Meaningful Connections	9
7	Chapter 7: The Value of Rest and Recovery	11
8	Chapter 8: Finding Joy in Simple Pleasures	13
9	Chapter 9: The Importance of Reflection	15
10	Chapter 10: The Art of Letting Go	17
11	Chapter 11: The Power of Gratitude	18
12	Chapter 12: The Benefits of Solitude	20
13	Chapter 13: The Art of Listening	22
14	Chapter 14: The Power of Purpose	24
15	Chapter 15: The Importance of Self-Compassion	26
16	Chapter 16: The Joy of Giving Back	28
17	Chapter 17: Embracing the Journey	30

1

Chapter 1: The Noise of Modern Life

In today's fast-paced world, we often find ourselves lost in the noise of constant activity and endless distractions. We are bombarded with information and expectations, leading to a state of perpetual busyness. This relentless pursuit of productivity can be exhausting and ultimately counterproductive. By recognizing the overwhelming noise around us, we can begin to appreciate the importance of slowing down and finding moments of silence in our daily lives.

The constant barrage of notifications, emails, and social media updates keeps us perpetually connected but often leaves us feeling disconnected from ourselves and others. This digital noise can create a sense of urgency and anxiety, preventing us from fully engaging with the present moment. By intentionally reducing our exposure to these distractions, we can reclaim our mental space and focus on what truly matters.

Moreover, the noise of modern life can lead to burnout and diminished well-being. The pressure to always be on the go and achieve more can take a toll on our physical and mental health. By embracing a slower pace, we can prioritize self-care and create a more sustainable approach to productivity. This shift allows us to replenish our energy and maintain a healthier balance in our lives.

Ultimately, the noise of modern life is a barrier to deep connections and meaningful experiences. When we are constantly rushing from one task to the next, we miss out on the richness of life and the opportunity to connect with others on a deeper level. By embracing the quiet hustle, we can achieve more by slowing down and fostering genuine connections.

2

Chapter 2: Embracing Stillness

Embracing stillness is a powerful antidote to the chaos of modern life. By cultivating moments of quiet and reflection, we can gain clarity and insight into our thoughts and emotions. Stillness allows us to step back from the constant busyness and reconnect with our inner selves. It provides the space to process our experiences and make intentional choices that align with our values.

Practicing stillness can take many forms, from meditation and mindfulness to simply sitting quietly and observing our surroundings. These practices help us develop a greater awareness of the present moment and cultivate a sense of calm. By regularly incorporating stillness into our routines, we can build resilience and enhance our ability to navigate life's challenges.

In addition to its mental and emotional benefits, stillness can also enhance our creativity and problem-solving skills. When we give ourselves the time and space to pause, we create the conditions for new ideas to emerge. This can lead to innovative solutions and fresh perspectives that we may not have discovered in the midst of constant activity.

Finally, embracing stillness can deepen our connections with others. By being fully present and attentive, we can engage in more meaningful conversations and build stronger relationships. Stillness allows us to listen more deeply and respond with greater empathy and understanding. In this way, the quiet hustle fosters a sense of community and belonging.

3

Chapter 3: The Power of Deep Work

Deep work is the ability to focus intensely on a task without distractions, leading to high-quality, meaningful output. In a world filled with constant interruptions, cultivating the skill of deep work is essential for achieving our goals and making a significant impact. By dedicating uninterrupted time to our most important tasks, we can produce work that is both innovative and impactful.

To practice deep work, we must create an environment that minimizes distractions and allows for sustained focus. This may involve setting boundaries with technology, creating a dedicated workspace, and establishing routines that support deep concentration. By prioritizing deep work, we can achieve a level of productivity that is both efficient and fulfilling.

In addition to its productivity benefits, deep work also contributes to our overall well-being. When we immerse ourselves in meaningful tasks, we experience a sense of flow and satisfaction. This state of deep engagement can lead to greater job satisfaction and a more fulfilling professional life. By committing to deep work, we can find greater purpose and fulfillment in our careers.

Furthermore, deep work allows us to build expertise and mastery in our chosen fields. By dedicating focused time to our craft, we can develop a deeper understanding and hone our skills. This pursuit of excellence not only benefits us individually but also contributes to the advancement of our industries and communities. In this way, the quiet hustle of deep work leads to lasting impact and personal growth.

4

Chapter 4: Cultivating Presence

Cultivating presence is about being fully engaged and attentive in the present moment. In a world where multitasking is often celebrated, the ability to be present can feel like a lost art. However, it is essential for building meaningful connections and experiencing life to its fullest. By practicing presence, we can enhance our relationships, improve our well-being, and achieve a greater sense of fulfillment.

One way to cultivate presence is through mindfulness practices that help us tune into our thoughts, emotions, and physical sensations. These practices teach us to observe our experiences without judgment and bring our attention back to the present moment. By regularly engaging in mindfulness, we can develop a greater awareness of our inner and outer worlds.

In addition to mindfulness, cultivating presence involves being fully engaged in our interactions with others. This means actively listening, making eye contact, and responding with empathy and understanding. By being present in our conversations, we can build stronger, more authentic connections and foster a sense of trust and respect.

Finally, cultivating presence allows us to fully appreciate the beauty and richness of life. When we are present, we notice the small details and moments of joy that might otherwise go unnoticed. This heightened awareness can lead to a greater sense of gratitude and contentment. By embracing the quiet hustle of presence, we can live more deeply and meaningfully.

5

Chapter 5: The Art of Single-Tasking

In a world that often values multitasking, the art of single-tasking can feel counterintuitive. However, focusing on one task at a time is a powerful way to enhance productivity and achieve better results. By giving our full attention to a single task, we can work more efficiently and produce higher-quality output. Single-tasking allows us to fully immerse ourselves in our work and achieve a state of flow.

To practice single-tasking, we must create an environment that minimizes distractions and supports focused work. This may involve setting boundaries with technology, organizing our workspace, and prioritizing our tasks. By eliminating interruptions and focusing on one task at a time, we can achieve a greater level of concentration and effectiveness.

In addition to its productivity benefits, single-tasking also contributes to our well-being. When we focus on one task at a time, we experience less stress and mental fatigue. This can lead to greater job satisfaction and a more balanced approach to work. By embracing single-tasking, we can achieve a more sustainable and fulfilling way of working.

Furthermore, single-tasking allows us to fully engage with our tasks and find greater meaning in our work. By dedicating our full attention to each task, we can develop a deeper understanding and appreciation for what we are doing. This sense of purpose and fulfillment can lead to greater job satisfaction and personal growth. In this way, the quiet hustle of single-tasking leads to a more meaningful and impactful life.

6

Chapter 6: Building Meaningful Connections

Building meaningful connections is essential for our well-being and personal growth. In a world that often prioritizes superficial interactions, cultivating deep and authentic relationships can feel challenging. However, meaningful connections are vital for our emotional and mental health, as well as our overall happiness. By investing time and effort into our relationships, we can create a support system that enriches our lives.

One way to build meaningful connections is by being present and fully engaged in our interactions with others. This means actively listening, showing empathy, and being open and honest in our communication. By prioritizing quality over quantity in our relationships, we can build stronger, more authentic connections that provide mutual support and understanding.

In addition to being present, building meaningful connections involves finding common interests and shared values. By engaging in activities and conversations that align with our passions and beliefs, we can connect with others on a deeper level. This sense of shared purpose and understanding can lead to more fulfilling and lasting relationships.

Finally, building meaningful connections requires vulnerability and authenticity. By being open about our thoughts, feelings, and experiences, we create space for others to do the same. This vulnerability fosters trust and deepens our connections with others. By embracing the quiet hustle of building meaningful connections, we can create a network of support and enrichment that enhances our lives.

7

Chapter 7: The Value of Rest and Recovery

Rest and recovery are essential for maintaining our well-being and achieving sustainable productivity. In a world that often glorifies constant activity and hustle, taking time to rest can feel counterproductive. However, rest is crucial for replenishing our energy, maintaining our health, and enhancing our overall performance. By prioritizing rest and recovery, we can achieve more in the long run.

One way to prioritize rest is by establishing regular routines that allow for downtime and relaxation. This may involve setting aside time for activities that help us recharge, such as reading, spending time in nature, or practicing mindfulness. By creating intentional rest periods, we can maintain a healthier balance between work and leisure.

In addition to regular routines, rest and recovery also involve getting adequate sleep. Quality sleep is essential for our physical and mental health, as well as our cognitive functioning. By prioritizing good sleep hygiene and establishing consistent sleep patterns, we can enhance our overall well-being and productivity.

Finally, rest and recovery allow us to reflect on our experiences and gain perspective. By taking time to pause and recharge, we can process our thoughts and emotions, leading to greater clarity and insight. This reflection can help us make more intentional choices and align our actions with our values. In this way, the quiet hustle of rest and recovery leads to a more balanced and fulfilling life.

8

Chapter 8: Finding Joy in Simple Pleasures

Finding joy in simple pleasures is a powerful way to enhance our well-being and experience greater fulfillment in our daily lives. In a world that often values material success
continue

Finding joy in simple pleasures is a powerful way to enhance our well-being and experience greater fulfillment in our daily lives. In a world that often values material success and external achievements, it's easy to overlook the small moments of happiness that can bring us true contentment. By shifting our focus to the simple pleasures in life, we can cultivate a greater sense of gratitude and joy.

One way to find joy in simple pleasures is by being present and fully engaged in the moment. This means taking the time to appreciate the beauty of nature, savoring a delicious meal, or enjoying a heartfelt conversation with a loved one. By slowing down and being mindful of these experiences, we can find greater satisfaction and contentment in our everyday lives.

In addition to being present, finding joy in simple pleasures involves recognizing and celebrating the small victories and accomplishments that often go unnoticed. This can include completing a challenging task, learning something new, or simply taking the time to relax and recharge. By acknowledging these moments, we can build a sense of accomplishment and self-worth.

Finally, finding joy in simple pleasures requires cultivating a mindset of gratitude and appreciation. By focusing on what we have rather than what we lack, we can develop a greater sense of contentment and happiness. This shift in perspective allows us to find joy in the ordinary moments of life and appreciate the richness of our experiences. In this way, the quiet hustle of finding joy in simple pleasures leads to a more fulfilling and meaningful life.

9

Chapter 9: The Importance of Reflection

Reflection is a powerful tool for personal growth and self-improvement. By taking the time to reflect on our experiences, we can gain valuable insights and learn from our successes and challenges. Reflection allows us to identify patterns in our behavior, recognize areas for improvement, and celebrate our achievements. By incorporating regular reflection into our routines, we can develop a deeper understanding of ourselves and make more intentional choices.

One way to practice reflection is through journaling, which provides a structured way to process our thoughts and emotions. By writing down our experiences and insights, we can gain clarity and perspective. Journaling also allows us to track our progress over time and identify patterns in our behavior. This practice can lead to greater self-awareness and personal growth.

In addition to journaling, reflection can also involve discussing our experiences with trusted friends or mentors. These conversations provide an opportunity to gain different perspectives and receive feedback and support. By engaging in open and honest dialogue, we can deepen our understanding of ourselves and our relationships.

Finally, reflection allows us to connect our actions with our values and goals. By regularly evaluating our choices and behaviors, we can ensure that we are living in alignment with our principles and aspirations. This intentional approach to life leads to greater fulfillment and a sense of purpose. In this way, the quiet hustle of reflection fosters personal growth and meaningful living.

10

Chapter 10: The Art of Letting Go

Letting go is an essential skill for achieving greater peace and contentment in our lives. In a world that often encourages us to hold on to possessions, grudges, and unrealistic expectations, learning to let go can be challenging. However, by releasing what no longer serves us, we can create space for new opportunities and experiences. Letting go allows us to move forward with greater clarity and freedom.

One aspect of letting go is decluttering our physical environment. By removing unnecessary possessions and organizing our spaces, we can create a more peaceful and functional living environment. This process can also have a positive impact on our mental and emotional well-being, as it allows us to let go of attachments to material items and focus on what truly matters.

In addition to decluttering our physical spaces, letting go also involves releasing emotional baggage and forgiving ourselves and others. Holding on to past hurts and grievances can weigh us down and prevent us from moving forward. By practicing forgiveness and compassion, we can free ourselves from the burden of resentment and create healthier relationships.

Finally, letting go requires accepting that we cannot control everything in our lives. By acknowledging our limitations and embracing uncertainty, we can reduce stress and anxiety. This acceptance allows us to focus on what we can control and make the most of the present moment. In this way, the quiet hustle of letting go leads to greater peace and fulfillment.

11

Chapter 11: The Power of Gratitude

Gratitude is a powerful practice that can transform our mindset and enhance our overall well-being. By focusing on the positive aspects of our lives and appreciating what we have, we can cultivate a greater sense of happiness and contentment. Gratitude shifts our perspective from what is lacking to what is abundant, leading to a more fulfilling and meaningful life.

One way to practice gratitude is by keeping a gratitude journal, where we regularly write down the things we are thankful for. This simple practice helps us become more aware of the positive aspects of our lives and fosters a sense of appreciation. By consistently focusing on gratitude, we can train our minds to notice and celebrate the good in our daily experiences.

In addition to journaling, expressing gratitude to others can strengthen our relationships and create a positive impact on those around us. By acknowledging and appreciating the efforts and kindness of others, we can build deeper connections and foster a sense of community. This practice of expressing gratitude can also lead to greater empathy and understanding.

Finally, cultivating a mindset of gratitude involves finding the silver lining in challenging situations. By looking for the lessons and opportunities in difficulties, we can develop resilience and a more optimistic outlook. This shift in perspective allows us to navigate life's ups and downs with greater grace and positivity. In this way, the quiet hustle of gratitude leads to a more

CHAPTER 11: THE POWER OF GRATITUDE

joyful and fulfilling life.

12

Chapter 12: The Benefits of Solitude

Solitude is a valuable practice that allows us to reconnect with ourselves and gain a deeper understanding of our thoughts and emotions. In a world that often prioritizes social interaction and external validation, spending time alone can feel uncomfortable or even lonely. However, embracing solitude can lead to greater self-awareness, creativity, and personal growth.

One benefit of solitude is the opportunity for introspection and self-reflection. By spending time alone, we can process our experiences and gain clarity on our values and goals. This introspection allows us to make more intentional choices and align our actions with our true selves. Solitude provides the space for deep thinking and self-discovery.

In addition to introspection, solitude can enhance our creativity and problem-solving skills. When we remove external distractions and create a quiet environment, we allow our minds to wander and explore new ideas. This mental space can lead to innovative solutions and fresh perspectives that may not emerge in the midst of constant social interaction.

Finally, embracing solitude can improve our relationships with others. By developing a strong sense of self and becoming comfortable with our own company, we can engage in more authentic and meaningful connections. Solitude allows us to recharge and replenish our energy, enabling us to be more present and attentive in our interactions with others. In this way, the

CHAPTER 12: THE BENEFITS OF SOLITUDE

quiet hustle of solitude fosters personal growth and deeper relationships.

13

Chapter 13: The Art of Listening

Listening is a crucial skill for building meaningful connections and fostering understanding. In a world that often prioritizes speaking and expressing opinions, the art of listening can feel undervalued. However, truly listening to others is essential for creating strong relationships and a sense of community. By practicing active listening, we can enhance our communication skills and build deeper connections.

Active listening involves being fully present and attentive in our interactions with others. This means putting aside distractions, making eye contact, and responding with empathy and understanding. By giving our full attention to the speaker, we demonstrate that we value their perspective and are genuinely interested in what they have to say.

In addition to being present, active listening involves asking open-ended questions and encouraging the speaker to share more. This practice helps us gain a deeper understanding of their thoughts and feelings and fosters a sense of trust and respect. By engaging in meaningful conversations, we can build stronger and more authentic relationships.

Finally, the art of listening requires practicing empathy and compassion. By putting ourselves in the speaker's shoes and acknowledging their emotions, we can create a supportive and understanding environment. This empathy helps us connect on a deeper level and fosters a sense of community and belonging. In this way, the quiet hustle of listening enhances our relationships

CHAPTER 13: THE ART OF LISTENING

and enriches our lives.

14

Chapter 14: The Power of Purpose

Having a sense of purpose is essential for achieving greater fulfillment and meaning in our lives. Purpose provides direction and motivation, guiding our actions and decisions. By aligning our lives with our values and passions, we can create a sense of purpose that drives us toward our goals and aspirations. This sense of purpose leads to greater satisfaction and a more meaningful life.

One way to cultivate a sense of purpose is by identifying our core values and passions. By reflecting on what truly matters to us and what brings us joy, we can gain clarity on our purpose. This process involves introspection and self-discovery, allowing us to connect with our true selves and define our vision for the future.

In addition to identifying our values and passions, living with purpose involves setting meaningful goals that align with our vision. These goals provide a roadmap for our actions and decisions, helping us stay focused and motivated. By pursuing our goals with intention and dedication, we can make progress toward our purpose and achieve a greater sense of fulfillment.

Finally, living with purpose requires embracing the journey and finding meaning in our daily experiences. By staying present and appreciating the small steps along the way, we can cultivate a sense of gratitude and joy. This mindset allows us to navigate life's challenges with resilience and optimism. In this way, the quiet hustle of purpose leads to a more fulfilling and meaningful

CHAPTER 14: THE POWER OF PURPOSE

life.

15

Chapter 15: The Importance of Self-Compassion

Self-compassion is a vital practice for maintaining our well-being and fostering personal growth. In a world that often emphasizes self-criticism and perfectionism, learning to be kind and understanding toward ourselves can be challenging. However, self-compassion allows us to navigate life's ups and downs with greater ease and resilience. By treating ourselves with the same kindness and empathy that we would offer to a friend, we can cultivate a healthier relationship with ourselves.

One way to practice self-compassion is by recognizing and challenging our inner critic. This involves acknowledging negative self-talk and reframing it with more supportive and compassionate language. By treating ourselves with understanding and forgiveness, we can build a stronger sense of self-worth and confidence.

In addition to challenging our inner critic, self-compassion also involves taking care of our physical and emotional needs. This means prioritizing self-care activities that nurture our well-being, such as exercise, healthy eating, and relaxation. By making self-care a regular part of our routine, we can build resilience and maintain a balanced and fulfilling life.

Finally, self-compassion allows us to embrace our imperfections and learn from our mistakes. By accepting that we are human and prone to errors, we

CHAPTER 15: THE IMPORTANCE OF SELF-COMPASSION

can approach challenges with a growth mindset and a sense of curiosity. This attitude fosters personal growth and development, allowing us to become the best versions of ourselves. In this way, the quiet hustle of self-compassion leads to a more compassionate and fulfilling life.

16

Chapter 16: The Joy of Giving Back

Giving back is a powerful way to create a positive impact in our communities and enhance our own sense of purpose and fulfillment. By contributing our time, skills, and resources to help others, we can build stronger connections and foster a sense of belonging. Giving back allows us to make a meaningful difference and experience the joy of helping others.

One way to give back is by volunteering for causes that align with our values and passions. Whether it's mentoring, supporting local charities, or participating in community service projects, volunteering provides an opportunity to connect with others and contribute to the greater good. By dedicating our time and energy to these efforts, we can make a lasting impact.

In addition to volunteering, giving back can also involve acts of kindness and generosity in our daily lives. This can include offering support to a friend in need, donating to a worthy cause, or simply being kind and considerate to those around us. These small acts of kindness can have a ripple effect, creating a positive impact on our communities.

Finally, giving back allows us to cultivate gratitude and a sense of purpose. By recognizing the positive impact we can make in the lives of others, we can develop a greater appreciation for our own blessings and opportunities. This mindset fosters a sense of fulfillment and joy, allowing us to experience the true meaning of giving. In this way, the quiet hustle of giving back leads to a

CHAPTER 16: THE JOY OF GIVING BACK

more meaningful and connected life.

17

Chapter 17: Embracing the Journey

Embracing the journey is about finding joy and fulfillment in the process of growth and self-discovery. In a world that often emphasizes achieving goals and reaching destinations, it's important to remember that the journey itself holds valuable lessons and experiences. By focusing on the present moment and appreciating the steps along the way, we can create a more meaningful and fulfilling life.

One way to embrace the journey is by setting intentions rather than rigid goals. Intentions allow us to stay focused on our values and aspirations while remaining flexible and open to new opportunities. This approach encourages us to enjoy the process and stay present, rather than becoming fixated on specific outcomes.

In addition to setting intentions, embracing the journey involves celebrating our progress and accomplishments, no matter how small. By acknowledging our efforts and growth, we can build a sense of confidence and motivation. This practice helps us stay positive and resilient, even in the face of challenges.

Finally, embracing the journey requires cultivating a mindset of curiosity and openness. By approaching life with a sense of wonder and a willingness to learn, we can find meaning and joy in our experiences. This attitude allows us to navigate life's ups and downs with grace and optimism. In this way, the quiet hustle of embracing the journey leads to a more fulfilling and meaningful life.

CHAPTER 17: EMBRACING THE JOURNEY

Book Description:

"**The Quiet Hustle: Achieving More by Slowing Down and Connecting Deeply**" is a transformative guide that challenges the conventional notion of hustle culture. In a world that glorifies constant busyness and productivity, this book offers a refreshing perspective on how to achieve more by embracing stillness, presence, and meaningful connections. Through 17 thoughtfully crafted chapters, readers will learn the power of deep work, the art of single-tasking, and the importance of rest and recovery. By slowing down and connecting deeply with themselves and others, readers will discover a more fulfilling and balanced approach to life. This book is a must-read for anyone seeking to find joy and purpose in the midst of a fast-paced world.

www.ingramcontent.com/pod-product-compliance
Lightning Source LLC
LaVergne TN
LVHW020739090526
838202LV00057BA/6131